PRINCEWILL LAGANG

Dating in the Spirit: A Christian Approach to Love

First published by PRINCEWILL LAGANG 2023

Copyright © 2023 by Princewill Lagang

All rights reserved. No part of this publication may be reproduced, stored or transmitted in any form or by any means, electronic, mechanical, photocopying, recording, scanning, or otherwise without written permission from the publisher. It is illegal to copy this book, post it to a website, or distribute it by any other means without permission.

Princewill Lagang asserts the moral right to be identified as the author of this work.

First edition

This book was professionally typeset on Reedsy.
Find out more at reedsy.com

Contents

1	The Foundation of Love	1
2	Preparing Your Heart and Mind	4
3	Building Healthy Foundations	7
4	Navigating Challenges and Temptations	10
5	Cultivating a Lifelong Love	13
6	Preparing for Marriage	16
7	Sustaining a Vibrant Christian Marriage	19
8	Navigating Parenting and Family Life	23
9	Growing Old Together	27
10	Embracing the Final Season	31
11	Facing Grief and Loss	35
12	Celebrating a Life Well-Lived	38

1

The Foundation of Love

Title: Dating in the Spirit: A Christian Approach to Love

In a world filled with diverse ideas about dating and love, it can be challenging to navigate the complex landscape of modern relationships while remaining true to your Christian faith. "Dating in the Spirit" is a journey into understanding how to approach dating, love, and relationships with a foundation deeply rooted in the principles of Christianity. In this first chapter, we will explore the fundamental aspects of love, its significance in our lives, and how to lay a strong spiritual foundation for your romantic journey.

Section 1: The Meaning of Love

Love, as defined in the Bible, is a central theme that transcends cultural boundaries, theological interpretations, and the passing trends of society. The Apostle Paul, in 1 Corinthians 13, beautifully describes love as patient, kind, not envious, not boastful, not proud, not rude, not self-seeking, not easily angered, and keeping no record of wrongs. It rejoices in truth and protects, trusts, hopes, and perseveres.

In understanding this biblical definition, we discover that love is not merely a fleeting emotion or infatuation but a profound and selfless commitment to another person's well-being. It is a force that should guide our actions and intentions, not only in romantic relationships but in all aspects of life.

Section 2: The Purpose of Love

Why is love so significant in the Christian context? Love is at the heart of Christianity; it is the driving force behind Jesus' teachings and actions. In the New Testament, Jesus encapsulated the essence of His teachings in two commandments: to love God with all your heart, soul, and mind, and to love your neighbor as yourself (Matthew 22:36-40). Love, therefore, is not just an option for Christians; it's a commandment.

In the context of dating, the purpose of love is not simply to find personal happiness or fulfillment, but to honor God and serve one another. A Christian approach to love places God at the center of the relationship, seeking to reflect His love in our interactions.

Section 3: The Role of the Spirit

The Holy Spirit plays a vital role in guiding our romantic endeavors as Christians. In John 14:16-17, Jesus promises to send the Holy Spirit as a helper and comforter who will be with us forever. This divine guidance becomes especially crucial in dating, as it enables us to discern God's will, make wise choices, and foster healthy, loving relationships.

The Spirit also empowers us to exhibit the qualities described in 1 Corinthians 13. It helps us to be patient, kind, and forgiving, even in the face of challenges. It allows us to love unconditionally and develop empathy and understanding towards our partner.

Section 4: The Biblical Perspective on Dating

While the Bible may not explicitly mention dating as we understand it today, it provides us with valuable principles for relationships. We find stories of courtship, marriage, and family dynamics throughout the Old and New Testaments, offering insights into how we should approach romantic relationships as Christians.

In this chapter, we'll lay the groundwork for a biblical perspective on dating, emphasizing the importance of purity, intentionality, and accountability. We'll explore how the principles of respect, communication, and discernment should guide our romantic pursuits, and how our relationships should reflect the love and grace of Christ.

In "Dating in the Spirit," we aim to equip you with the knowledge and spiritual wisdom to navigate the challenges of modern dating while remaining firmly rooted in your faith. As we delve deeper into this journey, you will learn how to build relationships that honor God, respect one another, and ultimately reflect the boundless love of the Creator.

2

Preparing Your Heart and Mind

Title: Dating in the Spirit: A Christian Approach to Love

Before embarking on a Christian approach to dating and love, it's essential to prepare your heart and mind. This chapter will guide you through the process of self-reflection and spiritual readiness to ensure you are in the right place to pursue romantic relationships in a way that aligns with your faith.

Section 1: Self-Examination

Before seeking a partner, it's crucial to engage in self-examination. In 2 Corinthians 13:5, the apostle Paul encourages believers to examine themselves to ensure they are in the faith. This principle is just as relevant when considering romantic relationships.

1. Identity in Christ: Start by understanding your identity in Christ. Realize that your worth is not defined by your relationship status, appearance, or achievements but by your relationship with God.

2. Past Relationships: Reflect on past relationships, seeking lessons learned from both successes and failures. Consider what you are looking for in a

partner and what you can bring to a relationship.

3. Personal Growth: Evaluate your spiritual, emotional, and personal growth. Are there areas in your life that need improvement or healing before you're ready to engage in a romantic relationship?

Section 2: Setting Godly Priorities

In Matthew 6:33, Jesus advises us to "seek first the kingdom of God and His righteousness, and all these things will be added to you." Before entering a romantic relationship, you should have a clear sense of your priorities, aligning them with your faith.

1. Spiritual Growth: Make your relationship with God your top priority. Dedicate time to prayer, Bible study, and spiritual growth to strengthen your foundation.

2. Values and Beliefs: Identify your core values and beliefs. What principles will guide your decisions and actions in a romantic relationship?

3. Godly Goals: Set godly goals for your future and your potential relationship. Consider how your relationship can be a vehicle for serving God and His kingdom.

Section 3: Seeking Accountability and Guidance

Ecclesiastes 4:9-10 emphasizes the value of having companions on your journey: "Two are better than one because they have a good return for their labor. If either of them falls down, one can help the other up."

1. Accountability Partner: Find a trusted Christian friend or mentor who can hold you accountable in your pursuit of godly relationships. Share your goals, concerns, and progress with them.

2. Parental Guidance: If possible, seek guidance from your parents or trusted family members. Their wisdom and experience can be invaluable in your dating journey.

3. Church Community: Engage in your church community and participate in activities that promote healthy relationships. You can find support, encouragement, and like-minded individuals who share your faith values.

Section 4: Cultivating Contentment

Contentment, as emphasized in Philippians 4:11-12, is crucial in preparing your heart and mind. "I have learned to be content whatever the circumstances. I know what it is to be in need, and I know what it is to have plenty. I have learned the secret of being content in any and every situation."

1. Single Life: Embrace your current season of singleness. Understand that being single is not a deficiency but an opportunity for personal growth and service to God.

2. Gratitude: Practice gratitude for the blessings in your life. A grateful heart fosters contentment and makes you more attractive as a potential partner.

3. Trust in God's Timing: Trust in God's timing for your romantic journey. Patience and faith are essential virtues in seeking a godly relationship.

Preparing your heart and mind is a foundational step in pursuing a Christian approach to love. This chapter has provided you with guidance on self-examination, setting priorities, seeking accountability, and cultivating contentment. With these principles in place, you will be better equipped to enter a romantic relationship with a heart and mind aligned with your faith.

3

Building Healthy Foundations

Title: Dating in the Spirit: A Christian Approach to Love

As you continue your journey to explore a Christian approach to dating and love, it's important to build a healthy foundation for your future relationships. This chapter delves into the key aspects of building such a foundation, emphasizing character development, communication, and setting boundaries guided by biblical principles.

Section 1: Developing Character

1. Fruit of the Spirit: Galatians 5:22-23 describes the "fruit of the Spirit" as love, joy, peace, patience, kindness, goodness, faithfulness, gentleness, and self-control. These qualities are not only essential in a Christian's character but also in the context of a healthy relationship.

2. Self-Awareness: Continue to develop self-awareness. Understand your strengths and weaknesses, your triggers, and your emotional responses. Self-awareness can help you cultivate humility, empathy, and patience.

3. Service and Sacrifice: A strong character involves a willingness to serve and sacrifice for the well-being of your partner. This selflessness is a reflection

of Christ's love for the Church (Ephesians 5:25).

Section 2: Effective Communication

1. Listening: Learn to listen actively and empathetically. Often, communication issues in relationships arise from misunderstandings or the failure to truly hear your partner's perspective.

2. Open and Honest: Encourage open and honest communication. Transparency is key to building trust in a relationship. Ephesians 4:25 advises, "Therefore each of you must put off falsehood and speak truthfully to your neighbor, for we are all members of one body."

3. Conflict Resolution: Understand the biblical approach to conflict resolution (Matthew 18:15-17). Approach conflicts with humility, a willingness to reconcile, and a focus on resolving issues rather than winning arguments.

Section 3: Setting Biblical Boundaries

1. Purity and Sexual Boundaries: Maintain purity in your relationship by setting clear sexual boundaries in line with biblical principles (1 Corinthians 6:18-20). These boundaries may include avoiding premarital sex and other physical expressions that could compromise your purity.

2. Emotional Boundaries: Establish emotional boundaries that protect your heart and the hearts of your partner. Guard against becoming overly emotionally invested too quickly, which can lead to heartache if the relationship doesn't progress as expected.

3. Time and Priorities: Be mindful of how you allocate your time. Your relationship should not take precedence over your relationship with God or other essential responsibilities. Matthew 6:33 encourages us to "seek first the kingdom of God."

Section 4: Shared Spiritual Growth

1. Prayer and Worship: Cultivate a shared spiritual life within your relationship. Pray together, worship together, and encourage each other's faith journeys.

2. Bible Study: Engage in regular Bible study as a couple. This not only deepens your understanding of God's Word but also provides an opportunity for spiritual growth together.

3. Accountability: Continue to seek accountability, both individually and as a couple. A supportive community can help you stay on the right path and encourage one another in your faith.

By focusing on character development, effective communication, biblical boundaries, and shared spiritual growth, you are building a strong foundation for a healthy and God-honoring relationship. This chapter provides practical guidance to ensure your relationship is firmly grounded in the principles of Christian love and faith.

4

Navigating Challenges and Temptations

Title: Dating in the Spirit: A Christian Approach to Love

Dating in the spirit is a journey that presents its share of challenges and temptations. In this chapter, we'll explore how to navigate these hurdles with wisdom and faith, ensuring your relationship remains grounded in Christian principles.

Section 1: Facing Temptations

1. Sexual Temptation: It's essential to acknowledge the presence of sexual temptation and prepare to address it. The Bible provides guidance on maintaining sexual purity, such as 1 Thessalonians 4:3-4, which instructs believers to avoid sexual immorality.

2. Worldly Influences: Recognize the impact of worldly influences on your relationship. Popular culture often promotes values that contradict Christian principles, so it's crucial to be discerning and resistant to these pressures.

3. Selfish Desires: Temptations can also arise from selfish desires, such as the desire for control, validation, or personal satisfaction. Reflect on the importance of selflessness in your relationship and consider the words of

Philippians 2:3: "Do nothing out of selfish ambition or vain conceit. Rather, in humility value others above yourselves."

Section 2: Building Trust and Overcoming Doubt

1. Trust in God: In moments of doubt and uncertainty, turn to your trust in God. Proverbs 3:5-6 advises, "Trust in the Lord with all your heart and lean not on your own understanding; in all your ways submit to him, and he will make your paths straight." Seek His guidance and wisdom.

2. Trust in Your Partner: Trust is a vital component of any relationship. Open, honest communication and consistent actions that align with your Christian values can help build and maintain trust in your relationship.

3. Overcoming Doubt: When doubt creeps in, address it directly with your partner. Share your concerns and work together to find solutions or reassurances. Remember that love "always trusts" (1 Corinthians 13:7).

Section 3: Communication and Conflict Resolution

1. Effective Communication: Continue to work on your communication skills. Clear, respectful, and compassionate communication is essential in overcoming challenges and resolving conflicts.

2. Conflict Resolution: Understand that conflicts will arise in any relationship. Approach them with a biblical perspective, seeking reconciliation and understanding rather than victory. Follow the principles outlined in Matthew 18:15-17 for resolving issues within your relationship.

3. Seeking Wisdom: When faced with challenging decisions or conflicts, seek wisdom from trusted Christian mentors, friends, or family members who can offer guidance and support.

Section 4: Strengthening Your Faith Together

1. Prayer and Devotion: Continue to nurture your shared spiritual life. Praying together and engaging in devotional practices can deepen your bond and provide guidance and strength during challenging times.

2. Community Support: Lean on your church community for support and encouragement. Share your challenges and seek prayer and advice from fellow believers who can walk with you through difficulties.

3. Perseverance: Remember that love is patient and perseveres (1 Corinthians 13:4-7). Commit to persevering through challenges, knowing that, with God's help, you can overcome them and grow stronger together.

Navigating challenges and temptations is an integral part of any relationship, but it becomes even more crucial when dating with a Christian approach. By remaining vigilant, building trust, communicating effectively, and strengthening your faith, you can overcome these obstacles and continue on your path toward a loving, God-centered relationship.

5

Cultivating a Lifelong Love

Title: Dating in the Spirit: A Christian Approach to Love

As you progress in your journey of dating in the spirit, it's time to explore how to cultivate a love that lasts a lifetime. This chapter focuses on the qualities and practices that help create a deeply fulfilling and enduring Christian relationship.

Section 1: Building Lasting Love

1. Companionship in God: A lifelong love is rooted in companionship with God. Continue to prioritize your individual relationships with God and seek to grow spiritually both independently and as a couple.

2. Selfless Love: Selflessness is a hallmark of lasting love. Continue to put your partner's needs before your own, as emphasized in Philippians 2:3-4: "Do nothing out of selfish ambition or vain conceit. Rather, in humility value others above yourselves."

3. Forgiveness: Forgiveness is a critical component of lasting love. Ephesians 4:32 encourages us to "be kind and compassionate to one another, forgiving each other, just as in Christ God forgave you." Cultivate a heart of forgiveness

in your relationship.

Section 2: Deepening Intimacy

1. Emotional Intimacy: Continue to foster emotional intimacy by sharing your thoughts, feelings, and dreams with your partner. Building a strong emotional connection strengthens your bond.

2. Spiritual Intimacy: Deepen your spiritual connection by praying together, studying the Bible, and serving together in your faith community. A shared spiritual life can provide a strong foundation for lasting love.

3. Physical Intimacy: While maintaining purity, nurture physical intimacy within the bounds of marriage. Ensure that your sexual relationship is an expression of love and unity, as advocated in Song of Solomon.

Section 3: Perseverance and Resilience

1. Weathering Storms: Every relationship faces challenges. To cultivate lasting love, you must be willing to persevere through the storms, drawing strength from your faith and from each other.

2. Resilience: Develop resilience as a couple. Be prepared to adapt to life's changes and challenges, knowing that love is about enduring through the highs and lows.

3. Seeking Professional Help: If your relationship faces significant challenges, consider seeking professional counseling or advice from your church community. There is no shame in seeking help when necessary.

Section 4: Commitment to Growth

1. Continuous Growth: Encourage continuous growth in your relationship.

Seek to learn and grow together, supporting each other's personal development and faith journeys.

2. Shared Dreams and Goals: Revisit and update your shared dreams and goals regularly. A sense of purpose and shared vision can fuel lasting love.

3. Building a Legacy: Consider how your love can leave a legacy of faith, love, and service to others. Your love story can be a testament to the enduring power of God's love.

A lifelong love is a beautiful testament to the transformative power of God's love in our lives. By continuing to build a foundation of selflessness, deepening intimacy, cultivating perseverance and resilience, and committing to growth, you can create a love that endures through the trials and joys of life.

6

Preparing for Marriage

Title: Dating in the Spirit: A Christian Approach to Love

In the journey of dating in the spirit, the ultimate destination for many couples is marriage. This chapter explores the steps and considerations for preparing for a Christian marriage based on love, faith, and commitment to God's plan.

Section 1: Seeking God's Guidance

1. Prayer and Discernment: Seek God's guidance through prayer and discernment. This is a significant decision, and it's essential to align your intentions with His will. Proverbs 3:5-6 reminds us to trust in the Lord with all our hearts and lean not on our understanding.

2. Counsel and Wisdom: Seek counsel from wise, godly mentors, pastors, or other couples who have experienced successful Christian marriages. Their insights can provide valuable guidance.

Section 2: Premarital Preparation

1. Pre-Marital Counseling: Consider undergoing pre-marital counseling

with a qualified Christian counselor or within your church. This process helps you navigate potential issues, explore your compatibility, and address areas that may need improvement.

2. Discussing Key Issues: Engage in open, honest discussions about key issues such as faith, finances, family planning, and personal values. Establish your mutual understanding and agreement on these matters.

3. Conflict Resolution Training: Enhance your conflict resolution skills by learning strategies for dealing with disagreements in a healthy and Christ-centered manner. Seek to create a harmonious atmosphere in your relationship.

Section 3: Godly Marriage Principles

1. Submission and Servant Leadership: Embrace the biblical principles of mutual submission (Ephesians 5:21) and servant leadership (Ephesians 5:25). These principles underpin a Christ-centered marriage, emphasizing love, respect, and partnership.

2. Love as Christ Loved: Continually strive to love one another as Christ loved the Church (Ephesians 5:25). This means sacrificial love, which places the well-being of your spouse above your own.

3. Communication: Maintain effective communication in your marriage. Keep the lines of communication open and commit to resolving conflicts through respectful dialogue.

Section 4: Navigating Challenges

1. Anticipate Challenges: Be prepared to face challenges in your marriage. Life can be unpredictable, but with a solid foundation of faith and love, you can navigate these challenges together.

2. Sickness and Health: Commit to supporting one another in sickness and health, as outlined in marriage vows. Encourage one another's physical and emotional well-being.

3. Lifelong Commitment: Remember that a Christian marriage is a lifelong commitment. Be ready to weather the storms and celebrate the joys together, knowing that your commitment is underpinned by your shared faith.

Section 5: Building a God-Honoring Marriage

1. Service and Ministry: Consider how you can serve together as a couple in your church and community. Your marriage can be a vessel for God's work, demonstrating His love and grace.

2. Prayer and Worship: Continue to prioritize prayer, worship, and spiritual growth as a couple. Nurture your spiritual connection and deepen your love for God and each other.

3. Marriage as a Witness: Recognize that your marriage can be a powerful witness to others. Your love and commitment can inspire and encourage those around you.

Preparing for marriage is a significant step in the dating journey, and it involves seeking God's guidance, engaging in pre-marital preparation, embracing godly marriage principles, and navigating challenges with faith and commitment. A Christian marriage is a lifelong partnership built on love, mutual respect, and dedication to God's plan.

7

Sustaining a Vibrant Christian Marriage

Title: Dating in the Spirit: A Christian Approach to Love

Congratulations on your journey from dating to marriage in the spirit! This chapter will explore how to sustain a vibrant Christian marriage, keeping God at the center of your relationship as you embark on this lifelong commitment.

Section 1: Prioritizing God in Your Marriage

1. Daily Devotion: Continue to make time for daily devotion, both individually and as a couple. Prayer and Bible study can strengthen your faith and your bond with one another.

2. Worship Together: Attend church services, engage in worship, and participate in spiritual activities together as a couple. This shared spiritual life keeps God at the forefront of your relationship.

3. Spiritual Growth: Commit to ongoing spiritual growth. Encourage and support each other's spiritual journeys, striving to become more Christ-like in your attitudes and actions.

Section 2: Maintaining Emotional Intimacy

1. Open Communication: Keep the channels of communication open. Regularly express your thoughts and feelings to each other, and actively listen to your spouse's concerns and joys.

2. Quality Time: Set aside quality time for one another. Date nights, weekend getaways, and other special moments help maintain emotional intimacy and strengthen your connection.

3. Supporting One Another: Be a source of emotional support for your spouse. In times of joy and sorrow, demonstrate your love and commitment by being there for each other.

Section 3: Nurturing Physical Intimacy

1. Purity and Faithfulness: Maintain your commitment to purity and faithfulness. Sexual intimacy should be a reflection of your love, unity, and commitment to each other within the bounds of your Christian marriage.

2. Romance and Affection: Continue to show love and affection in your relationship. Small gestures of love and romantic expressions can keep the flame of physical intimacy alive.

3. Open Communication: Discuss your physical needs, desires, and boundaries. Ensure you both feel comfortable and fulfilled in this aspect of your marriage.

Section 4: Resolving Conflict God's Way

1. Conflict Resolution: Approach conflicts with a Christ-like attitude. Seek to resolve issues with patience, humility, and forgiveness, always aiming for reconciliation (Matthew 18:15-17).

2. Seeking Wisdom: When facing difficult decisions or conflicts, seek wisdom from trusted mentors, pastors, or counselors. External guidance can provide fresh perspectives and solutions.

3. Prayerful Resolution: Pray together when facing significant issues in your marriage. Inviting God into the process can bring clarity, understanding, and healing.

Section 5: Embracing Life Changes Together

1. Adapting to Change: Be prepared to adapt to life's changes as a couple. Career shifts, family expansions, and other life events may require flexibility and support.

2. Support and Encouragement: Offer unwavering support and encouragement to your spouse. Celebrate their achievements, be there in times of adversity, and remember the importance of unity in facing life's changes.

3. Shared Dreams: Revisit and adjust your shared dreams and goals as your lives change. Adapt your vision to encompass the ever-evolving nature of your marriage.

Section 6: Leaving a Legacy of Love

1. Service and Ministry: Continue to seek opportunities to serve and minister together. Your marriage can be a powerful vessel for demonstrating God's love and grace to others.

2. Mentoring Others: Consider mentoring or providing guidance to other couples, especially those who are just starting their journey of dating and marriage. Your experience can be a valuable source of inspiration and support.

3. Leaving a Legacy: Keep in mind the legacy you want to leave. How will your love, faith, and commitment impact future generations and those around you? Strive to leave a legacy that glorifies God.

Sustaining a vibrant Christian marriage is a lifelong journey. By prioritizing God, maintaining emotional and physical intimacy, resolving conflict with Christ-like attitudes, embracing life changes together, and leaving a legacy of love, you can keep your marriage strong and centered on your shared faith.

8

Navigating Parenting and Family Life

Title: Dating in the Spirit: A Christian Approach to Love

As your Christian marriage progresses, one of the most profound journeys you may embark upon is parenting and family life. This chapter will explore how to navigate the challenges and joys of raising a family while keeping God at the center of your Christian home.

Section 1: Preparing for Parenthood

1. Prayer and Discernment: Seek God's guidance as you consider becoming parents. Pray for wisdom, discernment, and the ability to fulfill your roles as stewards of His gift of children.

2. Preparation: Engage in discussions about your parenting philosophies and strategies. Address important questions about discipline, values, and your approach to raising children.

3. Counsel and Support: Seek counsel and support from other Christian parents, mentors, and your church community. Learning from the experiences and insights of others can be invaluable as you prepare for parenthood.

Section 2: Parenting with Faith and Love

1. Spiritual Foundation: Establish a strong spiritual foundation for your family. Incorporate daily prayer, Bible study, and worship into your family routine. Teach your children the importance of faith and guide them in their spiritual journeys.

2. Teaching God's Values: Educate your children about God's values and principles. Instill in them the importance of love, kindness, humility, and service to others through both your words and actions.

3. Family Devotions: Set aside time for family devotions. These moments can be powerful opportunities to connect as a family and grow together in your faith.

Section 3: Discipline and Guidance

1. Biblical Discipline: Implement discipline in your family based on biblical principles. Ephesians 6:4 advises fathers not to provoke their children to anger but to bring them up in the discipline and instruction of the Lord.

2. Consistency: Maintain consistency in your discipline and guidance. Children thrive in an environment where expectations are clear and boundaries are consistent.

3. Communication: Create an open environment where your children feel comfortable discussing their concerns, questions, and fears. Use communication as a tool for guidance and mentorship.

Section 4: Balancing Work and Family

1. Prioritizing Family Time: Strive to prioritize family time over work or other commitments. Your presence and involvement in your children's lives

are essential for their emotional and spiritual well-being.

2. Support System: Lean on your support system when needed. Family, friends, or your church community can offer assistance and relief, ensuring that you maintain a balanced family life.

3. Quality Time: Focus on quality, not just quantity. Make the most of the time you spend with your children, ensuring that it is filled with love, guidance, and meaningful interaction.

Section 5: Raising Children in Faith

1. Lead by Example: Model a strong Christian faith in your daily life. Your children will learn from your actions and attitudes, so strive to be an example of love, humility, and faith.

2. Nurturing Individual Faith: Recognize that your children may have unique spiritual journeys. Encourage them to ask questions, explore their faith, and develop their personal relationship with God.

3. Prayer for Your Children: Dedicate time to pray for your children's well-being, faith, and future. Commit their lives and spiritual growth to God in your daily prayers.

Section 6: Building a Loving Christian Home

1. Service and Ministry: Engage in service and ministry as a family. This can be a powerful way to demonstrate God's love and cultivate a sense of purpose and unity in your home.

2. Family Traditions: Establish family traditions that reflect your Christian values. These traditions can create strong bonds and provide a sense of belonging for your children.

3. Legacy of Love: Strive to leave a legacy of love, faith, and service to others. Your Christian home can be a source of inspiration and guidance for generations to come.

Navigating parenting and family life as a Christian couple is a sacred journey. By preparing for parenthood, parenting with faith and love, offering discipline and guidance, balancing work and family, raising children in faith, and building a loving Christian home, you can create a nurturing environment that reflects God's love and grace.

9

Growing Old Together

Title: Dating in the Spirit: A Christian Approach to Love

As you journey through life, your Christian marriage will experience the full spectrum of joys, challenges, and changes. In this chapter, we will explore the art of growing old together with grace, faith, and enduring love.

Section 1: A Lifetime of Memories

1. Reflection and Gratitude: Take time to reflect on the journey you've shared as a couple. Express gratitude for the blessings, challenges, and growth you've experienced together.

2. Preserving Memories: Invest in preserving your memories. Compile photographs, journals, and keepsakes that tell the story of your life together.

3. Celebrating Milestones: Celebrate milestones, anniversaries, and special moments that mark your shared history. These celebrations strengthen your bond and create cherished memories.

Section 2: Enduring Love

1. Unconditional Love: Reflect on the meaning of unconditional love. Your love for each other should be characterized by patience, kindness, forgiveness, and selflessness, as described in 1 Corinthians 13.

2. Forgiveness: Continue to practice forgiveness. Be quick to forgive, as Christ forgave you (Colossians 3:13). Holding on to grudges can erode the foundation of your relationship.

3. Growing Deeper: As you grow older together, seek to deepen your love and commitment. Continue to prioritize your marriage and prioritize one another.

Section 3: Health and Well-Being

1. Prioritizing Health: Pay attention to your health and well-being. Staying healthy and active allows you to enjoy your life together and serve God in your later years.

2. Supporting Each Other: Be a source of support and encouragement for one another's physical and emotional health. Help each other maintain a balanced and healthy lifestyle.

3. Navigating Challenges: Address health challenges together with patience and grace. Sickness and the aging process can be trying, but your love can serve as a source of strength and comfort.

Section 4: Relationships with Adult Children and Grandchildren

1. Maintaining Connection: Maintain a close connection with your adult children and grandchildren. Support and encourage their lives, and be a source of wisdom and guidance.

2. Family Traditions: Create family traditions that include your extended

family. These traditions can provide opportunities for unity and bonding across generations.

3. Prayer for Future Generations: Continue to pray for your family's well-being and faith. Your prayers can have a lasting impact on the spiritual growth of your children and grandchildren.

Section 5: Facing Life Changes

1. Adapting to Change: Embrace the changes that come with aging, retirement, and evolving life circumstances. Your flexibility and adaptability will be crucial as you grow old together.

2. Rediscovering Each Other: Rediscover each other as you enter new phases of life. Find joy in your shared interests and the time you have to explore new activities and experiences.

3. Planning for the Future: Discuss and plan for your future as you age. This includes considerations about living arrangements, end-of-life care, and financial security.

Section 6: Leaving a Legacy of Love

1. Service and Ministry: Continue to serve and minister as a couple, even in your older years. Your example of love and faith can be a powerful testament to God's enduring grace.

2. Mentoring Others: Offer guidance and mentorship to younger couples who are on their own journey of love and faith. Share your wisdom and experiences to inspire and support others.

3. Legacy of Love: Consider the legacy you wish to leave for your family and those around you. Strive to be a source of inspiration and a living testament

to God's love.

Growing old together is a sacred journey, marked by a lifetime of shared experiences, enduring love, and the continued presence of God's grace. By celebrating your memories, maintaining an enduring love, focusing on health and well-being, nurturing your relationships, facing life changes with grace, and leaving a legacy of love, you can journey into your later years with faith and grace.

10

Embracing the Final Season

Title: Dating in the Spirit: A Christian Approach to Love

As your Christian marriage reaches its later years, it's important to embrace the final season of your journey with faith, love, and a deep sense of fulfillment. In this chapter, we will explore how to navigate the challenges and joys of this stage with grace and a focus on your eternal destination.

Section 1: Reflecting on Your Journey

1. Gratitude and Reflection: Take time to express gratitude for the life you've built together. Reflect on your journey as a couple, acknowledging the blessings, challenges, and growth you've experienced over the years.

2. Treasured Memories: Relive treasured memories by looking through photographs, journals, and keepsakes that document your life together. Sharing these memories with your spouse can be a source of joy and connection.

3. Celebrating Your Love: Celebrate your enduring love and commitment. Plan special moments to mark significant milestones and anniversaries,

reinforcing the depth of your love for each other.

Section 2: Deepening Your Faith

1. Spiritual Growth: Continue to prioritize your spiritual growth. Deepen your relationship with God through daily prayer, Bible study, and worship. As you grow closer to God, you'll also grow closer to each other.

2. Eternal Perspective: Embrace an eternal perspective. Recognize that your final season is a prelude to the eternal life that awaits you. Your faith will be your guiding light on this journey.

3. Legacy of Faith: Consider the legacy of faith you wish to leave for your family and those around you. Your love and faith can inspire others and serve as a testament to God's grace.

Section 3: Navigating Health Challenges

1. Prioritizing Health: Continue to prioritize your health and well-being. Stay active, eat well, and ensure that you're taking care of your physical and emotional health.

2. Support and Care: Be a source of support and care for your spouse in times of health challenges. Your unwavering love and assistance can provide comfort and strength.

3. Acceptance and Grace: Practice acceptance and grace in the face of health challenges. Your faith can help you navigate these difficulties with a sense of peace and purpose.

Section 4: Cherishing Family and Relationships

1. Maintaining Connection: Keep your connections with your adult children

and grandchildren strong. Support and encourage their lives and be a source of wisdom and guidance as they navigate their own journeys.

2. Family Traditions: Continue to embrace and create family traditions that include your extended family. These traditions can provide opportunities for unity and bonding across generations.

3. Prayer for Future Generations: Pray for your family's well-being and faith, even in your later years. Your prayers can have a lasting impact on the spiritual growth of your children and grandchildren.

Section 5: Facing Life Changes with Grace

1. Adapting to Change: Embrace the changes that come with aging, retirement, and evolving life circumstances. Your flexibility and adaptability will be crucial as you navigate the final season of your journey together.

2. Rediscovering Each Other: Rediscover each other in this phase of life. Find joy in shared interests and in the time you have to explore new activities and experiences together.

3. Planning for the Future: Discuss and plan for your future as you age, including considerations about living arrangements, end-of-life care, and financial security.

Section 6: Leaving an Eternal Legacy

1. Service and Ministry: Continue to serve and minister, even in your later years. Your example of love, faith, and endurance can be a powerful testament to God's grace.

2. Mentoring Others: Offer guidance and mentorship to younger couples and individuals who are on their own journey of love and faith. Share your

wisdom and experiences to inspire and support others.

3. Eternal Legacy: Consider the eternal legacy you wish to leave. Strive to be a source of inspiration and love for your family and all those whose lives you've touched. Your journey will continue in the presence of God for all eternity.

Embracing the final season of your Christian marriage is a unique and sacred journey, marked by a lifetime of shared experiences, enduring love, and the continued presence of God's grace. By reflecting on your journey, deepening your faith, navigating health challenges with grace, cherishing family and relationships, facing life changes with flexibility, and leaving an eternal legacy, you can embrace this season with faith and a profound sense of fulfillment.

11

Facing Grief and Loss

Title: Dating in the Spirit: A Christian Approach to Love

Grief and loss are inevitable parts of the human experience, and they often become more prominent in the later stages of life. In this chapter, we will explore how to navigate these challenging emotions within the context of your Christian marriage, relying on faith, love, and the comfort of God's presence.

Section 1: Acknowledging Grief

1. Understanding Grief: Grief is a natural response to loss. Acknowledge that it is normal and healthy to experience grief when facing the loss of loved ones, health, or other significant aspects of life.

2. Sharing Grief: Share your grief with your spouse. Open, compassionate communication can help you both process your emotions and support each other through the grieving process.

3. God's Comfort: Turn to God for comfort. Psalm 34:18 reminds us that "The Lord is close to the brokenhearted and saves those who are crushed in spirit." Seek solace in your faith and your relationship with God.

Section 2: Coping with Loss

1. Support Systems: Lean on your support system, which may include family, friends, or your church community. Allow others to offer their love, prayers, and assistance during times of loss.

2. Grief Counseling: Consider seeking grief counseling or therapy if you find it difficult to cope with loss. A trained professional can provide guidance and support during this challenging time.

3. Healthy Coping Mechanisms: Focus on healthy coping mechanisms, such as exercise, meditation, or creative outlets, to help you navigate grief. These activities can provide solace and relief.

Section 3: Supporting Each Other

1. Emotional Support: Be a source of emotional support for your spouse as you both navigate grief and loss. Create an atmosphere of empathy, understanding, and patience.

2. Mutual Healing: Understand that the process of healing may differ for each person. Allow space for your spouse to grieve in their own way and time, and offer mutual support.

3. Prayer for Strength: Pray for strength and guidance during these difficult times. Together, seek God's presence and solace through prayer and spiritual practices.

Section 4: Embracing Hope and Resilience

1. Maintaining Hope: Hold on to hope, knowing that God's love and grace are ever-present. Find comfort in the assurance that even in moments of loss, God has a purpose and plan.

2. Resilience: Cultivate resilience as a couple. Grief and loss can be profoundly challenging, but with your faith and love as anchors, you can weather these storms and find strength in each other.

3. Leaving a Legacy of Resilience: Your journey through grief and loss can also leave a legacy of resilience and faith for your family and those around you. Share your experiences and your capacity to find hope and healing.

Section 5: Preparing for the Future

1. Discussion and Planning: As you age, discuss end-of-life matters with your spouse. Consider creating or updating your will, making advance care plans, and discussing your preferences for end-of-life care.

2. Legacy of Faith: Continue to nurture your legacy of faith. The final chapter of life provides opportunities to share your faith and trust in God's plan with your loved ones.

3. Peaceful Transitions: Embrace the idea of peaceful transitions. Your Christian faith can bring peace and hope, not only in the midst of grief but also in the face of the unknown as you prepare for eternity.

Facing grief and loss in the later stages of life can be especially challenging, but with faith, love, and the support of your spouse and your Christian community, you can navigate these emotions and find comfort in God's presence. Grief, though painful, can also become a testament to the enduring power of love and faith in your Christian marriage.

12

Celebrating a Life Well-Lived

Title: Dating in the Spirit: A Christian Approach to Love

In the final chapter of your Christian journey together, it's time to reflect on your life, celebrate the love, faith, and experiences you've shared, and prepare to transition into the eternal embrace of God's love. This chapter will guide you on how to celebrate a life well-lived with grace, gratitude, and a profound sense of fulfillment.

Section 1: Gratitude and Reflection

1. Counting Blessings: Take time to count your blessings. Reflect on the myriad ways in which God has been present in your lives, both individually and as a couple.

2. Treasured Memories: Share and revisit treasured memories. Review photographs, journals, and keepsakes that document the highlights of your life together.

3. Expressing Gratitude: Express your gratitude for your spouse and for the journey you've shared. Use this time to tell each other what you appreciate most about your life together.

Section 2: Celebrating Your Love

1. Renewal of Love: Renew your commitment to love and cherish each other. A reaffirmation of your love can serve as a beautiful capstone to your journey.

2. Family and Friends: Consider having a celebration of love with family and friends. This gathering can provide an opportunity for loved ones to express their love and gratitude.

3. Words of Encouragement: Share words of encouragement with each other. Reflect on your love, your enduring commitment, and the strength of your faith.

Section 3: Embracing God's Grace

1. Prayer and Worship: Continue to prioritize prayer and worship as a couple. These spiritual practices can provide comfort and strength as you prepare for the next phase of your journey.

2. Comfort in God's Presence: Find comfort in the presence of God. Psalm 23:4 reassures us: "Even though I walk through the darkest valley, I will fear no evil, for you are with me." Lean on your faith as you transition to eternity.

3. Leaving a Spiritual Legacy: Your final season offers an opportunity to leave a spiritual legacy for your loved ones. Share your faith and trust in God's eternal plan, demonstrating the peace that comes with a life well-lived in Christ.

Section 4: Preparing for Eternal Life

1. Transition to Eternity: Embrace the transition to eternity with faith and hope. Remind each other of the promise of eternal life that awaits those who believe in Christ.

2. End-of-Life Plans: Continue discussions about end-of-life matters, ensuring that your wishes are known and documented. This includes considerations about living arrangements, advanced directives, and your spiritual legacy.

3. Celebrating God's Love: Find solace in the knowledge that you will soon be in the presence of God's eternal love. This transition is not an end but a continuation of your journey in the embrace of divine love.

Section 5: Leaving a Legacy of Love and Faith

1. Service and Ministry: Consider the legacy of love and faith you wish to leave behind. Your journey, marked by love, faith, and service to others, can inspire and guide future generations.

2. Mentoring Others: Offer your wisdom and experiences to younger couples and individuals, inspiring them to live a life of faith and love. Your journey can be a source of encouragement and support.

3. Eternal Legacy: Your legacy of love and faith doesn't end with your earthly life. It continues into eternity, serving as a testament to the enduring power of God's love.

Celebrating a life well-lived as a Christian couple is a sacred journey marked by gratitude, love, faith, and the presence of God's grace. By reflecting on your blessings, celebrating your love, embracing God's grace, preparing for eternal life, and leaving a legacy of love and faith, you can transition into the next phase of your journey with a sense of peace and fulfillment.

Book Summary: "Dating in the Spirit: A Christian Approach to Love"

"Dating in the Spirit: A Christian Approach to Love" is an insightful and comprehensive guide that takes readers on a journey through the various stages of Christian dating and marriage, offering wisdom, guidance, and spiritual insights for building lasting, meaningful relationships.

The book consists of twelve chapters, each dedicated to a different aspect of the dating and marital experience, all grounded in Christian principles and values.

The journey begins with Chapter 1, where readers are introduced to the concept of dating with a spiritual foundation. It emphasizes the importance of faith and love as the building blocks of a Christ-centered relationship.

Chapters 2 to 6 guide readers through the stages of dating, from finding a potential partner to preparing for marriage. The book delves into the qualities and practices that help create a strong foundation for a lifelong Christian love, including companionship in God, selfless love, forgiveness, deepening intimacy, and perseverance.

Chapter 7 focuses on sustaining a vibrant Christian marriage, offering guidance on maintaining emotional and physical intimacy, resolving conflicts, and weathering life's changes together.

Chapter 8 addresses the transition into parenthood and family life, discussing how to nurture your relationship, raise children with faith and love, and navigate the challenges of balancing work and family.

Chapter 9 explores how to cope with grief and loss within the context of a Christian marriage, emphasizing the importance of support, resilience, and faith during difficult times.

Chapter 10 prepares readers to face the final season of life with grace and gratitude, navigating health challenges, cherishing family and relationships, and leaving a legacy of love and faith.

Chapter 11 dives into the process of celebrating a life well-lived, helping couples reflect on their journey, renew their love, and find comfort in God's presence as they prepare to transition into eternity.

The final Chapter 12 offers guidance on preparing for eternal life, emphasizing the promise of God's love and leaving a spiritual legacy for future generations.

Throughout the book, readers are encouraged to prioritize faith, love, and service to others, fostering a sense of purpose and connection in their relationships. "Dating in the Spirit" is a powerful resource for Christians seeking to build and sustain strong, loving, and God-centered relationships at every stage of life. It combines practical advice with spiritual wisdom to provide a comprehensive guide to navigating the complexities of dating, marriage, and the challenges and joys that come with them, all within the context of a deep and abiding faith in God.

www.ingramcontent.com/pod-product-compliance
Lightning Source LLC
LaVergne TN
LVHW010438070526
838199LV00066B/6070